Some Kids Just Can't Sit Still!

Sam Goldstein

Illustrations by Allie DeSisto

Some Kids Just Can't Sit Still!

Published by
Specialty Press, Inc.
300 Northwest 70th Ave.
Plantation, FL 33317

For information about our books, including a complete catalog,
please write to us, call 1-800-233-9273 or visit us on the Internet at
www.addwarehouse.com

ISBN-13: 978-1-886941-73-1
ISBN-10: 1-886941-73-4

Printed in China

This book is dedicated to my friends Ian and Tanner and children everywhere.

Although learning about and understanding ourselves

isn't always easy, it's always helpful.

Some kids just can't sit still,
They wiggle and jiggle, fidget and flop!

They don't mean to do it,
They just can't stop.

Out on the playground
They want to play.
But with just one game or friend
It's so hard to stay.

No one else really cares
It's no bother they chat.
But they just won't play
With someone like that.

With homework they promise,
To sit and be neat.
To finish it all
Glued to their seat.

But homework is boring,
It's just no fun.
They would rather be playing
Out in the sun.

At dinner they're late,
Sloppy or slow.
A drink is spilled
And dad yells, "oh no!"

They don't mean to do it,
They promise once more.
But no one believes them,
They've promised before.

They get into things
That aren't their own.
They run, jump and shout
When mom's on the phone.

"Stay out of my room,
Get out of my stuff!"
Big brother yells,
"I've had more than enough!"

Every once in a while
They get angry too.
Then they just refuse
When it feels too hard to do.

Mom says take a bath,
Clean your room, do it now!
But oh no they don't want to,
So they tell her and how.

Late at night in their beds
They feel sad and cry.
They don't look for trouble,
They really do try!

Problems, problems, problems
Wherever they go.
Does this story sound
Like someone you know?

Do you fidget and flop,
Can't sit still in one place?

Is your mind running quickly
On a long distance race?

Do you just have to talk
When teachers say no?

Do you start lots of things
And finish them slow?

Do you need things exciting
To keep your mind in one place?
Do you move without thinking
On an endless fun chase?

If this describes you,
Please don't be sad.
Other kids have this problem too.
You're not ill, sick or bad.

You've got a condition
As some people do.
It's called ADHD,
And its part of you.

It means that you need
Life to be fast and exciting.
You want to sit still
But getting up is oh so inviting.

A visit to the doctor,
He says you're not sick.
But there are things we can do
That will help you real quick.

Your brain's a bit different,
It works much too fast.
You act without thinking.
Sitting calmly doesn't last.

You rush through your work,
Taking tests seems so easy.
Then you're told much is wrong
And your stomach feels queasy.

You know what to do,
But don't do what you know.
The good news is
We can help you be happy and grow!

Your mom and dad
Place a chart by the phone.
To help you learn habits
And do things on your own.

Brush your teeth, comb your hair,
Come to dinner on time.
No more yelling or fighting,
Now things will be fine.

The doctor may tell you,
Take this pill every day.

It won't change who you are,
But may help in more than one way.

These things will help you stay calm.
Your work will get done.

You'll sit still and focus
And have more time for fun.

You can stop, look and listen,
Have a plan when you play.

Finish all of your school work
And succeed every day.

You're feeling much better,
Now you have hope.

You wake up with a smile,
Now you can cope.

You've got to keep trying
Till you find something fun.

An activity you can stick with,
Maybe soccer's the one!

You start lots of things,
You've learned not to quit.

You've got to hang in there,
That's the answer, that's it!

In class you can't miss,
Your work is just great.
You know you can do it,
You're not even late.

Your teacher helps
To make work easy for you.
Lets you talk, move and question
Gives you fun things to do.

You're making more friends
In school and out.
Now kids really like you,
You just want to shout!

Even big brother
Has nice things to say.
He knows how hard you're trying
Each and every day.

The best part of all,
Is how great you feel.
You succeed every day,
And know it's for real.

Your parents, teachers and doctors
All do their part.
But it's your work and effort,
That's made a new start.

So now that you know
This thing called ADHD.

There's much we can do.
It's easy you see.

With everyone's help
You know lots more than before.

It's just ADHD,
And nothing more!

Tips for Parents

Words are powerful tools. They can change ideas and shape behavior. They can play a significant role in helping children understand themselves better and become active participants in any treatment process. This volume can help de-stigmatize a problem that your child experiences. This book can open lines of communication and provide your child with a logical, non-blaming understanding of Attention Deficit Hyperactivity Disorder (ADHD). To use this book effectively, I suggest the following:

- It may be worthwhile reading the book once all the way through and then reading it again with the child. In the course of reading the book, your child may also want to stop and comment about a picture or something described in the text. Keep in mind the purpose of this book is to provide information, as well as open dialogue.

- This book is directed at young children. I suggest you read the book to your child.

- In situations in which your child and siblings are in conflict, attempt to have an older sibling read the book to your child as well.

- This book is not recommended to replace talking to your child about this important issue. Rather, it is my hope that it serves as a catalyst to open lines of communication.

As parents we all want the very best for our children. We often feel stressed and sometimes hopeless as we observe our children struggling, particularly when we are uncertain what more we can do to help. It is my hope that this book will provide a framework to build hope and help motivate your child to become an active participant in the ADHD treatment process.

Resources

Adamec, C. & Gwinnell, E. (2000). *Mom's with ADD: A Self-Help Manual.* Taylor Trade Publishing.

Barkley, R. (2000). *Taking Charge of ADHD: The Complete Authoritative Guide for Parents.* New York, NY: Guilford.

Brooks, R., & Goldstein, S. (2007). *Raising a Self-Disciplined Child.* New York, NY: McGraw-Hill.

Brooks, R., & Goldstein, S. (2001). *Raising Resilient Children.* New York, NY: McGraw-Hill.

Brown, T.E., (2005). *Attention-Deficit Hyperactivity Disorder, The Unfocused Mind In Children and Adults* (Yale University Press)

DuPaul, G., & Stoner, G. (2003). *ADHD in the Schools* - 2nd Edition. New York, NY: Guilford Publishers.

Goldstein, S., Brooks, R., & Weiss, S. (2004). *Angry Children, Worried Parents: Seven Steps to Help Families Manage Anger.* Plantation, FL: Specialty Press.

Goldstein, S., Brooks, R. & Hagar, K. (2003). *Seven Steps to Help Your Child Worry Less: A Family Guide.* Plantation, FL: Specialty Press.

Jensen, P.S. (2004). *Making the System Work for Your Child with ADHD.* New York, NY: Guilford.

Lavoie, R. (2005). *It's So Much Work To Be Your Friend.* New York, NY: Simon and Schuster Publishers.

Mather, N. & Goldstein, S. (1998). *Overcoming Underachieving: An Action Guide to Helping Your Child in School.* New York, NY: Wiley.

Parker, H.C., & Goodstat, A. (1998). *Put Yourself In Their Shoes: Understanding Teenagers with Attention Deficit Hyperactivity Disorder.* Plantation, FL: Specialty Press.

Phelan, T. (2003). *1-2-3 Magic: Effective Discipline for Children 2-12.* Parentsmagic, Inc.

Wilens, T.E. (2004). *Straight Talk About Psychiatric Medications for Kids.* New York, NY: Guilford Press.

Zentall, Sydney S. (2006). *ADHD and Education: Foundations, Characteristics, Methods and Collaboration.* Pearson Press.

About the Author and Illustrator

Dr. Sam Goldstein is a psychologist and author of twenty-five books.
He can be reached at www.samgoldstein.com

Allie DeSisto works on a farm in Rhode Island
and illustrates in the off-season. She can be
reached at alassandra.desisto@gmail.com

Thanks to Allyson and Ryan Goldstein for their help with this story.